Mystical Patterns
Coloring Book

Mystical Patterns

Coloring Book

Create your own stunning designs

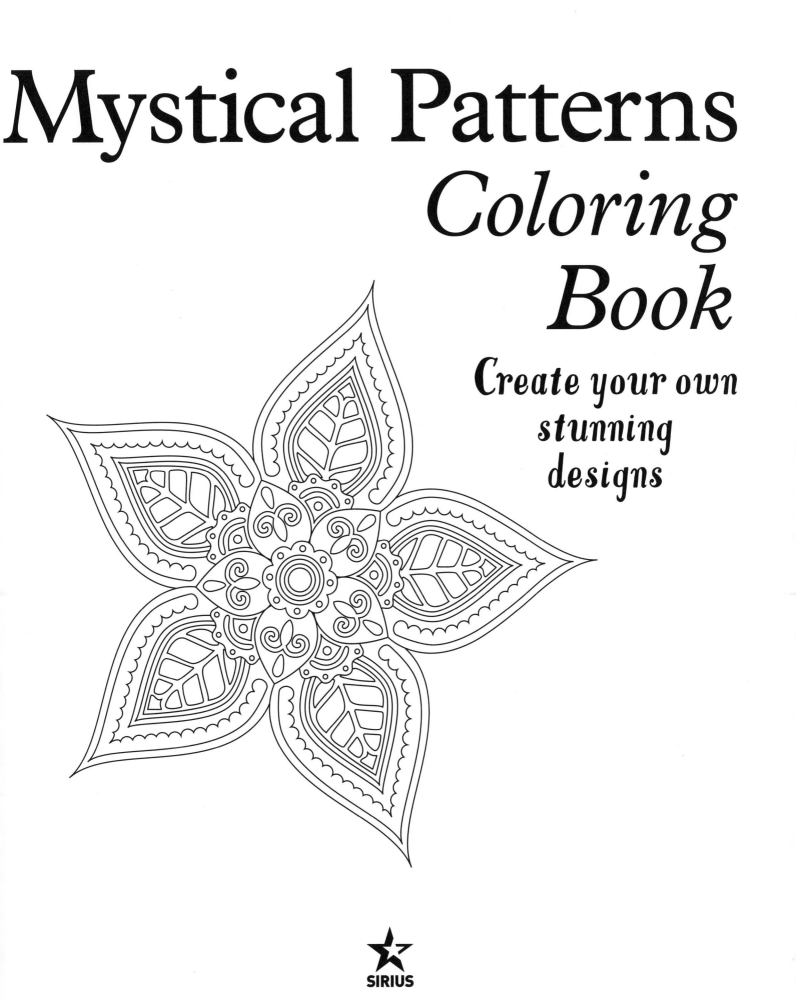

SIRIUS

This edition published in 2023 by Sirius Publishing, a division of
Arcturus Publishing Limited,
26/27 Bickels Yard, 151–153 Bermondsey Street,
London SE1 3HA

Copyright © Arcturus Holdings Limited

ISBN: 978-1-3988-3667-9
CH011159NT
Supplier 29, Date 1023, PI 00005349

Printed in China

Introduction

A host of fabulous mystical patterns awaits your coloring magic. There are many mandalas, the repeating circular patterns that represent a spiritual journey in Hinduism, Buddhism, Shinto, and Jainism. Carl Jung believed that they represented an individual's complete personality and encouraged his patients to create their own mandalas. Or you can color the curls and swirls of paisley, where the main shape might represent a mango, a teardrop, or even a kidney, and is known as a "boteh" or "buto," or "flower" in Persian. Most famously found in Kashmir, in northern India, it appears on fine shawls and other textiles. Other patterns are based on water and the peaceful repeating of ripples or waves, and organic shapes including shells and flowers. All you need is an hour or so of your time, a peaceful spot and your favorite coloring implements, be they pencils, pens, or markers.

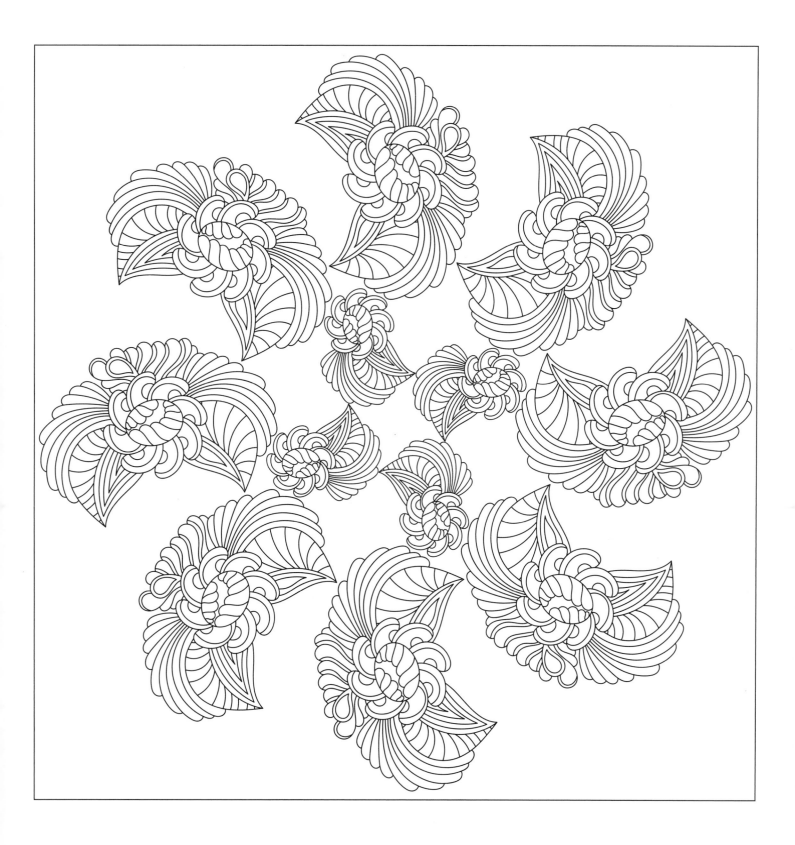